Tomorrow's Africa

Conference Report

Edited by John Gwynn

Hansib Publishing

Published in 1995 by Hansib Publishing Limited
Third Floor, Tower House, 141-149 Fonthill Road, London N4 3HF England

Introduction Copyright © Oxfam, 1995

Printed in the United Kingdom by Redwood Books, Trowbridge, Wiltshire

British Library Cataloguing-in-Publication Data
A catalogue record for this book is available from the British Library

ISBN 1-870518-39-X

Contents

Publisher's Foreword 5

Introduction 7

Acknowledgements 9

Keynote speech by Odhiambo Anacleti 11

Keynote speech by Dr Ekei Etim 15

Keynote speech by Abdul Rahman Babu 20

Keynote speech by Dr Fatima Babiker Mahamoud 27

Keynote speech by Pauline Green MEP 28

HEALTH ISSUES IN AFRICA 29

WHY AID? 31

AFRICAN WOMENS' MOVEMENTS 35

EQUAL NEWS ACCESS FOR AFRICA 39

AFRICAN DEBT 43

REFUGEES AND DISPLACED PEOPLE 45

DEMOCRATISATION IN AFRICA 47

DISABILITY 51

ARMED CONFLICT IN AFRICA 54

AFRICAN LITERATURE AND DEVELOPMENT 59

MOZAMBIQUE AND ANGOLA 61

MINING IN AFRICA 65

DEVELOPMENT AID TO TARGET CONFLICT PREVENTION 67

REGIONAL ECONOMIC COOPERATION 71

TIGRAY - A NEW HOPE 74

HOW TO TAKE CAMPAIGNING ACTION ON AFRICA 77

Publisher's Foreword

Tomorrow's Africa, billed as a *Call to Action by African Voices*, brought to the heart of London a new approach to the problems, perspectives and potentials of a continent. Held at the London School of Economics on January 15 1994, organised by Oxfam and sponsored by the *Caribbean Times (incorporating African Times),* this truly momentous conference provided a platform for some of Africa's finest minds, thereby creating a powerful think tank, which addressed realistically, constructively and practically, some of the intractable problems that impede progress on the continent. This down to earth conference has, moreover, kept its promise to translate its conclusions into action, a very necessary antidote to the usual heady and romantic rhetoric that we have so far been accustomed to.

It is often forgotten that Africa has existed for centuries and that it produced some of the world's finest civilisations. Pre-colonial Africa fed, clothed and housed its peoples comfortably. Its agriculture, before it was wrecked by colonial mono-culture, compared with the best of the period in Europe and Asia.

Africa's environment and wildlife was also of an enviable quality, with the correct balance struck by a continent aware that continents overpowered nature at their peril.

There is much to learn from the past as Africa struggles to undo the terrible damages inflicted by colonial domination. We at Hansib, publishers both of *Caribbean Times (incorporating African Times)* and this conference report, are very proud to have been associated throughout with this most realistic and productive conference on the continent's future which enabled representatives of Africa's greatest asset - its thinkers - hammer out workable proposals in the first stage of a peaceful revolution to feed, clothe, house, educate and shelter the people of Africa, and to give them the health, security and stability that is their inalienable right.

Keynote speaker panel (left to right) Dr Ekei Etim, Pauline Green MEP, Fatima Babiker Mahamoud, Odhiambo Anacleti and Abdul Rahman Babu

Photo courtesy: Ken Mears

Introduction

Much has been achieved at a grass roots level in Africa, and opportunities are presenting themselves today in the form of economic and political reform which hold out the prospect of a new era of development in Africa.

Oxfam works in 25 African countries and has offices in most of them. In 1993, Oxfam spent £36 million, almost half of all its overseas expenditure, funding 1,200 community-based programmes across the continent to support the efforts of poor people, especially women, to secure sustainable livelihoods, fundamental rights and access to basic services. Oxfam is working with people in a process of change in which people identify their common goals and work together to empower themselves, working with many African non-governmental organisations to emphasise that it is African people themselves who have the right and the capacity to take control of their own development and future.

But international pressure to repay Africa's debts has led to economic "adjustments" which have imposed huge social costs whilst manifestly failing to generate recovery. Also, faced with disastrously low commodity prices and unfair terms of trade, most African countries have had to cut social services to the poorer sections of the community, resulting in increased suffering.

Despite increasing pressure to actively address the resulting welfare gaps, Oxfam remains committed to its main long-term role of assistance for the efforts of poor people to take part in and influence the decision-making processes that affect their lives, including supporting these communities to voice their shared concerns internationally.

The *Tomorrow's Africa* conference was part of this advocacy programme, aimed at promoting policy changes nationally and internationally to reduce injustice, one of the fundamental causes of African poverty.

It was an event with international significance and there is much in this report of the conference workshops which will challenge many readers. By bringing together a wealth of experience and knowledge from such a wide variety of groups and individuals concerned with African affairs, the *Tomorrow's Africa* conference put down a milestone at this turning point in African history. As a new development panorama opens across Africa with both unprecedented opportunities and unprecedented obstacles this document forms a unique contribution from an African perspective to the debate about the way forward. It is an essential source for all those involved or interested in that debate.

The challenge remains, and the inspiration of listening to fresh and critical African voices must only be matched by our willingness to address the range of actions suggested throughout this document.

Acknowledgements

Oxfam's very grateful thanks go to Arif Ali and all the staff at the *Caribbean Times (incorporating African Times)* and Hansib Publishing for their support and sponsorship for the *Tomorrow's Africa* conference and this Conference Report.

Our heartfelt thanks also go out to each of the keynote speakers and workshop leaders whose insights, enthusiasm and generosity made the conference the spectacular success it was.

My own thanks go out to the conference planning group of Miti Ampoma, Bernie Ashmore, Kathleen Christie, Disni Jaysuriya, Natasha Theobald, and Caroline Whitfield. Thank you also to Ian Taylor and Caroline Whitfield for their help preparing this document.

Finally our thanks also go to all the participants who came from far and wide to listen to the range of African voices gathered under one roof. May the memory of it always inspire us to further action!

John Gwynn
Oxfam
December 1994

Keynote speech by

Odhiambo Anacleti

Africa Communications Officer for Oxfam

Today's conference on *Tomorrow's Africa* has brought together Africans, experts in Africa and African friends to call for action from the international community to give Africa and its citizens a hope for a better future. The conference is taking place at a very pertinent time in so far that, as Africa is adjusting to the new changes brought about by the cold war period there is a greater need now than ever to remind ourselves of some salient facts concerning the continent.

Keynote speaker Odhiambo Anacleti, Africa Communications Officer for Oxfam

Photo courtesy: Ken Mears

First, it is important to remember that Africans are constantly working for sustainable livelihood and upholding of their human rights amidst external injustice which is beyond their control. There is no time when this struggle stopped.

Second, there is a need to emphasise the fact that the African crisis, well-known to many of us through the media, has not made all Africans into starving beggars who are in permanent need for salvation from outside. The crisis has certainly brought about a lot of suffering, but has not conquered Africa.

Third, it is important to make it known that the current problem in Africa is not lack of know-how but rather a result of an internal institutional balance in which there is too much reliance on the state as the principle mechanism of change and development within an unjust world order which causes and sustains poverty, which in turn causes distress and suffering.

Fourth, is the fact that the world is currently more ideological than ever before in so far that the northern fundamentalist belief in the free market is trying to bulldoze all other ideologies, regardless of

"Remember that Africans are constantly working for sustainable livelihood and upholding of their human righs amidst external injustice which is beyond their control. There is no time when this struggle stopped"

11

their historical roots, with the consequence that some very reactionary ideologies are beginning to re-emerge in Africa.

The main purpose of this conference, which has been organised by Oxfam with generous support from the *Caribbean Times*, is to provide an opportunity for Africans and friends of Africa to add their voices to the call made by Oxfam in its report *Africa Make or Break, Action for Recovery*. That report called for the international community to:

☐　Reduce Africa's debt burden in order to release resources for investment in its people and economic recovery

☐　Increase aid flows to support peace and democracy and recovery

☐　Improve Africa's trading prospects

☐　Reform structural adjustment programmes to provide a framework for economic recovery and poverty alleviation

☐　Strengthen the role of the UN to improve its ability to respond to humanitarian emergencies and to prevent and mediate in conflicts.

It is my hope that this objective will be achieved and I wish you a good day of serious deliberation leading to positive action.

Keynote speaker Fatima Babiker Mahamoud addresses the conference alongside Oxfam's Odhiambo Anacleti (centre) and Abdul Rahman Babu

Photo courtesy: Ken Mears

Keynote speaker Dr Ekei Etim, Director of the Pioneer Agency for Development in Africa

Photo courtesy: Ken Mears

Keynote speech by

Dr Ekei Etim

Director of the Pioneer Agency for Development in Africa (PADA)

This conference is unique in calling upon Africans to debate the best way forward for Africa. NGOs, Western governments and media have for too long exploited the situations in Africa. Their activities have distorted situations in Africa and have reinforced a one-sided stereotyped view of the so-called African condition.

PADA questions the sources and methods of disseminating information. The population, for example, is not exploding as Westerners suggest. 25 out of the 53 countries have a population of less than five million. Africa has resources to sustain a large population and requires a large population to sustain industrialisation. Far from being a homogeneous entity, Africa is a place of immense diversity with over 2000 ethnic groups, yet documentaries constantly show just one of these groups, the Masai people. Images persist that show Africans as starving and malnourished, living in war zones. This is not an image peculiar to Africa nor does it apply to the whole 600 million people who inhabit the continent.

Western governments have acted to keep Africa disunited by exploiting weaknesses and by playing one country against another. Western institutions and governments have collaborated with African elites to syphon public funds into Swiss and other bank accounts. In condemning African governments for corruption, Western governments must accept that they are also corrupt, as no attempt is made to track down and return this money.

So-called western experts have also failed Africa in prescribing solutions to Africa's problems in terms of economic growth, structural adjustment programmes, foreign investment, aid and debt write off.

These measures fail in two ways:

1   Priority is not given to the impact on development within Africa. Solutions designed to enable African countries to pay back money owed to the IMF are bound to fail.

2   The root cause of problems are seldom addressed and the cultural, historical and political setting in which these solutions are imposed is ignored.

"The key to African development problems lies within, not outside the continent. Africa should stop paying for loans it has paid five times over and stop producing goods such as cash crops that are of no benefit to Africans themselves"

The key to African development problems lies within and not outside the continent. Africa is enormous. It has a land mass that could accommodate the US four times over; it is capable of producing 130 times its current yield and 40 per cent of the world's hydro-electric supplies, 30 per cent of the world's known reserves of uranium, 50 per cent of its gold and 40 per cent of its platinum, to name a few.

African leaders have consistently failed to govern and manage their economies, putting self-interest above national or public interest. They have accepted the quickest ways of making money through collaboration with the West and have not addressed the basic needs of the people. Governments should target basic needs instead of engaging in heavy spending on arms, the building of a replica of the basilica, or new capital cities. They should provide food, education and medical care and establish sound infrastructures, including good roads, communication networks, electricity and clean water.

Africa should stop paying for loans they have paid five times over and stop producing goods such as cash crops that are of no benefit to Africans themselves. Instead governments and peoples of Africa should put Africa first and take full advantage of the natural wealth, huge domestic markets and the continent's diversity.

Regional co-operation has failed in the past but there is an urgency to re-think development and move forward. A study in 1986 revealed that the PTA (Preferential Trade Agreement) sub-region imports

$6 billion worth of 450 product groups and imports identical products worth $4 billion. There is more intra- African trade going on that has been documented, but large potential trade is missed because countries are unaware that products are manufactured within the Continent.

The attempt of Ivory Coast to host a Trade Fair of goods manufactured in South Africa is a welcome event. Business will no doubt flourish between the two countries, and the cost and inconvenience involved for people attending will be considerably lower than if the fair was held in Europe.

The way forward is for Africans to work together and identify common interests. Regional co-operation is a sure way to develop, offering a sound foundation for sustained development. The treaty establishing the African Common Market in 1991 is rather too elaborate. Simple joint ventures should be explored. The last stage to the common market should be handled first to facilitate trade. (This stage envisages the setting up of an African Monetary Union, establishment of an African Central Bank and creation of a single African currency). Countries are already manufacturing and they need a medium of exchange now and not later. The smooth exchange of goods within the continent will speed up development, creating employment and giving people incomes to spend. The Afro-currency should be the weighted value of the relatively strong currencies in all the sub-regions. African governments must be committed to backing such a currency because currencies are the tools used to trade and control monetary affairs.

"Governments and peoples of Africa should put Africa first and take full advantage of the natural wealth, huge domestic markets and the continent's diversity"

One cannot deny the fact that there are key problems with regional co-operation but unity of purpose is the key to future development. The essence of development is to generate domestic income and demand for the production of goods and services. Increase in income will generate domestic savings. Foreign capital and investment supplements the domestic, not the other way round.

17

However, diversification to produce what is really needed and manufacturing of goods have to go hand in hand with political participation of the people and peaceful co-existence in Africa. Politics and economics are intrinsically linked.

The questions concerning the lives of the African people should not be left in the hands of Westerners. A nation decides its own future: a nation turns inward for strength and a sense of direction. Domestic factors have to be explored alongside international factors. The campaigns of NGOs must be questioned. They should address trading practices and rules which have encouraged exploitation of Africa. The rules of origin, safeguard clauses and agreements such as the concluded Uruguay Round of GATT have been tools used to distort African economies. This conference must put its full weight behind removing barriers to international trade. This conference must also support the move for an African Common Market because of the markets for goods and services that will be created. By doing so we might just be able to replace starving begging Africans with those who are beaming with confidence and are contributing positively in the international political and economic system.

Tigrayan cotton traders at the sharp end of unfair world trade practices
Photo: Jenny Matthews/Oxfam

Keynote speech by

Abdul Rahman Babu

commentator on African affairs and former
Minister for Economic Planning in Tanzania

Most of the world is rapidly moving ahead economically and socially except Africa and some parts of Latin America. What is the reason for Africa to remain as a permanently stagnant part of the world? Is there something inherently wrong with Africa and if so what is it? The reality is that there is absolutely nothing wrong except that the rest of the developing world has discovered that the only way to move forward is first of all to abandon the primitive colonial economic model left behind by the departing imperial powers. This model, which is predominant in the entire sub-saharan Africa, is our undoing and unless it changes to a more realistic one, Africa will be reduced to a fourth-world status.

What is wrong with the colonial economy? The colonial model, by its nature, is so structured that it does not promote the development of the productive forces or the expansion of the home market. If anything, it hampers both. Nor is it sufficiently equipped to benefit from the world trade to which it is historically tied from a position of extreme weakness. The first, i.e. the productive forces and home market, is necessary for earning the foreign exchange to import technology to modernise and accelerate internal development. Colonial economies are condemned to benefit from neither.

This colonial model has been based on the myth of "export-led" growth, as if African economic bases were properly structured to benefit from external exposure. It took thirty years and many millions of deaths by poverty to prove that the whole theory was based on a grand illusion. It did not work under colonialism and it is not working now.

The currently new and fashionable myth is the so-called SAP

Keynote speaker Abdul Rahman Babu
Photo courtesy: Ken Mears

"The colonial model was based on the myth of export-led growth. It took thirty years and many millions of deaths by poverty to prove that the whole theory was based on a grand illusion. It did not work under colonialism and it is not working now"

(Structural Adjustment Programme) enforced by "conditionality". This new myth, enforced by the most powerful post-war imperial agencies, the World Bank and the IMF, is based on the concept of "sound money". Whilst this may make sense in a wholly monetarised economy, to impose such a policy on economies which are only partially monetarised, i.e. on the subsistence economies of Africa, is attempting an impossible task. Yet this is exactly what Africa is condemned to do, at considerable cost to human life, mangled economies and loss of sovereignty.

African economic planners and strategists have, regrettably, accepted these damaging myths as workable propositions simply because, in the logic of conventional economic reasoning, they make sound economic sense. Criticism was limited to the unfavourable world economic order and they recommend cosmetic changes to "suit African conditions". They indulge in text book economics, thereby limiting their vision to changes in form but not in essence.

To see a different Africa of tomorrow will be an uphill task but not an impossible task. First, economic planners and decision makers must realise that while the rest of the world is on the move, Africa is stuck in a blind alley. Then they must be convinced that African nations must be elevated to an independent national economy by moving away from producing what is not consumed at home and consuming what is not produced at home, to an economy that produces principally for home consumption. They must be convinced that the satisfaction of the needs of millions upon millions of Africans must determine production. It may not be easy to convince them of this obvious truth since most of them have developed a vested interest in the status quo, but we must never give up, because the lives of millions of Africans are at stake.

Secondly, a strategy to achieve the objectives of a self-sustaining and independent economy must be formed: beginning by identifying in concrete terms what is to be rejected before proposing new solutions. Africans must loudly reject the colonial economies characterised by the following:

(a) Dependence on the industrialised world for development
(b) Excessive use of socially necessary labour in the production of useless goods for export instead of for home human and development needs
(c) Reliance on export of primary commodities which face continuous price deterioration thereby weakening capacity for capital accumulation (i.e. saving for further investment)
(d) Unproductive use of borrowed money, which entails debt servicing at criminally high interest rates
(e) Poor energy policies that make countries dependent on oil imports thereby depleting already meagre foreign exchange earnings
(f) Finally accept that all of this is taking place within an irrational world economic order which Africa cannot change from its position of weakness.

After discarding this model, a new one must be devised that is applicable to the concrete conditions of African societies. The ultimate objective is to create a good society, not for a few at the top, but one which will encompass all of the people. As a first step, that process must begin by making available enough food, decent housing and clothing to ensure stability and social harmony.

Promoting these objectives creates job opportunities in abundance. Modernising food production entails advancing to intensive farming and ranching, fisheries, poultry, dairy farming and so on. Hundreds of thousands of jobs will be created and new skills learnt.

Housing construction industry goes side by side with the expansion of the construction industry, which means developing capacity for building the economic and social structure. Development of the textile industry, principally for home consumption at affordable prices, opens up almost unlimited opportunities for job creation and skills. To be socially beneficial, all these projects must be labour intensive- to include as many people as possible in income generation thereby expanding domestic demand and widening the tax base. These are just a few examples of how to step-by-step move away from total dependence on foreign trade. Once the internal social and economic base is soundly founded, a sound foreign trade policy can be implemented taking into account what can be produced more advantageously for the global market place - not export of primary commodities but export of processed and manufactured goods, adding value to commodities and promoting of new skills.

But all this cannot be attained by pursuing conventional economic mechanisms. The key to economic and social success lies in relying on the social power rooted in African traditional culture. In the immediate aftermath of independence, this social power spontaneously mobilised itself in the euphoria of gaining sovereignty and national self-esteem. In Tanzania, for example, in the first two years of independence, people voluntarily and enthusiastically built ten thousand kilometres of roads throughout the country. They built health centres, schools, social centres. This was social power in action, inspired by the spirit of nation building.

Then came the economic planners and they killed that spirit and undermined social power.

"Africans must dare to think strategically!"

In China, described by the *Economist* recently as the fastest growing economy, unprecedented in world history, most of the country's success is dependent on social power. This power is said to manifest itself in three ground-level development processes that are vital to China's growth: a boom in home building, the spread of rural township enterprises and a rapid rise in human capital through self-study.

What can be learnt from the experience of Africa and China is that the roots of economic, technological and ultimately political power are social. Recreating new social power must be the primary motive force to move away from the colonial economy dependent on the production of coffee, tea, and tobacco, none of which is edible in times of hardship. But as we know, the creation of social power is negated by the SAP, conditionality and the economists who condone the whole imperialist conspiracy. They promote unemployment when employment is needed; they destroy health services and educational institutions when there is a need for healthy and educated people. Such policies are economically and socially illogical and they negate everything that is essential for awakening and mobilising social power. Africans must change course for their very survival and dare to think strategically.

"The key to economic and social success lies in social power rooted in African traditional culture"

**Keynote speakers
(left to right) Fatima
Babiker Mahamoud,
Abdul Rahman Babu
and Odhiambo Anacleti**

Photo courtesy: Ken Mears

Extracts surviving from the keynote speech by

Dr Fatima Babiker Mahamoud

President of the Association of Sudanese Academics and Researchers (UK), Advisor to Africa World Review, and Associate Professor of Political Economy and Development at South Bank University, London

This post cold war era is a time of ideological opportunity, a time for Africans to speak out and take control of the approach to African issues.

Up until now there has generally been a lack of empowerment with regard to deciding upon and implementing solutions at grassroots level. A balance must be reached between theory and practice, between an understanding of the problems and action taken.

In many instances women bear the full force of problems arising from poverty but are not in a position to influence decisions made that radically affect their lives. Women's subjugation is a global phenomenon although the form it takes and the extent to which it is tolerated differs from nation to nation and region to region. In Muslim states, the Quran, Hadith and Sharia reinforce a natural order that sidelines women.

However the silencing of women's voices not only dismisses the needs of half the population; it reinforces a bias that prevents so-called solutions from realistically meeting the needs of the people. Women as the home makers and child carers are in a prime position to identify "grassroot" problems and evaluate the likely success of community/regional initiatives. There is need for a holistic liberation to address the issues important to both men and women.

As womens' views are seldom listened to or even voiced, it is

"This post cold war era is a time of ideological opportunity, a time for Africans to speak out and take control of the approach to African issues"

important for World Bank/IMF policies to focus on the impact on women, health, education and children.

There currently exists a dichotomy between socio-economic factors and historical-cultural power structures. There is a need for a pan-African and possibly a global womens' movement so that the basic needs of women are treated as an essential and integral part of the needs of a community as a whole. Whilst the concerns of women may differ from region to region, their subjugation is a problem that brings all women together and so should be tackled as a whole.

Radio Douentza, Mali's first solar powered radio station, a powerful voice for women, backed by Oxfam

Photo: James Hawkins/Oxfam

Simultaneously there is a need for truly liberating movements for men leading towards a rebalancing of masculine and feminine qualities and full recognition of the contribution that all people play in all aspects of living and relationships.

Summary surviving of keynote speech by

Pauline Green MEP

Leader of The European Parliamentary Labour Party

Pauline Green MEP gave an exposition of Europe's current relationship with Africa economically and politically. The speech analysed the role that the then forthcoming European Elections had to play in offering opportunities to influence European relationships with Africa.

Pauline Green MEP did not speak from detailed notes, so regrettably no further material from her speech is available.

HEALTH ISSUES IN AFRICA

Health is an integral part of development. As long as African countries face dire economic conditions they will continue to have the worst health care systems. What options do African countries have to ensure that they provide health care for people without being dependent on aid? Aid is too fragmented and based on short term planning, rather than providing long term solutions to those that require it most, such as rural people.

Aid fails to empower the poor because it is not meant to. Its role is to create dependency, not self-sustained development. The sooner African governments realise this the better.

As northern governments continue to put significant resources into AIDS research, it is northern governments, not African people themselves, who have succeeded in putting AIDS on the agenda of African governments, while it is well-known that other common diseases continue to kill people in Africa.

Whereas AIDS has been defined as a "real problem", why are so many funds committed to education and control without an equal amount being put into containing infections? Why is being HIV+ an immediate death sentence in Africa whereas in the North HIV+ individuals can live for 10 years? There is a major debate concerning the choice between, on the one hand, allocating scarce resources to containing infection for those who are already sick, and on the other to allocating them to preventive work.

African countries should escape from the dependency of aid loans and repayments and organise health provision at village level by putting people, not government machinery, in charge. In such a

"Aid fails to empower the poor because it is not meant to. Its role is to create dependency, not self-sustained development. The sooner African governments realise this, the better"

"bottom-up" approach doctors, nurses and village-based communities can identify ways of financing the forms of health care that the community deems suitable.

One suggestion in the workshop was for African governments to divert some of the funds allocated for training of highly qualified professionals who expect huge salaries, and instead opt for a community-based doctor and nurse system. The suggestion was rejected for two reasons: first, that it implies an assumption that the poor do not deserve the best (but do they have the best in the current system where they never see a doctor?); secondly, that bottle-necks would occur making training and higher medical education a rare commodity. The conflicting views remained unresolved!

The final conclusions of the workshop were that African governments should manage their money better, develop their regions with particular attention to the rural populations, and pay qualified personnel in health services more attractively to avoid their migration abroad. No one should expect people who spend years getting qualified to be "patriotic" and remain when they can hardly afford to look after their families. No African government can impose a "purdah" on its educated elite: if they do not value them, they will leave and go where they are valued.

The workshop leader was Ravai Marindo-Ranganai who works in medical demography at the London School of Hygiene and Tropical Medicine, specialising in infant, child and maternal morbidity and mortality in Zimbabwe and health behaviour amongst minority ethnic groups. She previously lectured in sociology at the University of Zimbabwe.

WHY AID?

Has aid helped or crippled Africa? Africa's performance signifies a problem: income has declined by one per cent per year for a decade, literacy levels and school enrolments are the lowest globally, and it maintains the fastest population growth rate.

Has the problem been not enough aid? Would the problems have been worse without aid, or would they have been better with more aid? Conversely, has aid helped to cause the problems, or have issues such as later independence, corrupt dictatorships, dependence on commodities and resulting debts, or difficult natural environments been other factors?

Has aid been of the wrong kind? Bad aid projects are characterised by costing a lot, involving imports (e.g. the cost of pumps has risen by six hundred per cent), requiring expensive management, using unfamiliar or inappropriate technologies, ignoring economic and social situations, and not involving participation. Military assistance always brings net losses, as do aid programmes in the form of loans.

Aid that is "tied" to the purchase of goods and services from the donor country is less valuable, and technical assistance has often proved to be very questionable.

The overall impact of large sums of aid often undermines coherence of planning at governmental level. Problems include: multiplicity of donors (e.g. one country had sixty-nine donors and six hundred aid programmes in the 1980s); aid "fashions" such as trickle-down theories, industry-led, privatisation or basic needs; encouraging imports of western technologies.

"Unless the context of the international economy is put right, no amount of aid can help"

At another level, the result of loans from the IMF and the World Bank is that these multilateral institutions interfere in a range of national policies, particularly in areas which have great economic and environmental impact.

"Has aid helped or crippled Africa?"

The phenomenon of "aid sickness" attacks the immune system, that is to say the capacity of a country to run itself. The symptom is that no activity is undertaken without aid backing. So who is to blame for aid sickness? African governments encourage aid, mostly because they are bankrupt and have to seek all available funds. For some it clearly offers openings for corruption.

Aid projects can undermine African governments' abilities to run their own countries by "poaching" staff with offers of better salaries. In general, the poorer the country, the more aid it needs, but the more damage aid can do.

By comparison with bad aid, good aid is characterised by being low cost, involving fewer imports, having low management needs, high participation, and ensuring that social and economic needs are considered, especially those of women. Good aid is long term, reliable, consistent, coordinated amongst donors, and "enabling".In general good aid is targeted in sectors open to "enablement" such as health and education, and bad aid often applies to sectors such as agriculture, industry, and large construction projects.

"In general good aid is targeted in sectors open to 'enablement' such as health and education"

A number of questions remain. Would Africa be better off without aid - other than debt relief with no strings attached? Can aid be redesigned to be useful and not harmful? Should aid be discouraged in certain sectors? Should more aid be channelled through Non-Governmental Organisations(NGOs) - African and Northern? Do NGOs project the right image of Africa in trying to get more aid for themselves - how do they get more aid or debt relief without showing the "need"?

The workshop determined that: aid should be more effectively used to benefit ordinary Africans; NGOs should be used more, especially

African ones; aid should be participative, reaching grassroots communities; aid should strengthen, not weaken, African governments' capacity to achieve objectives; aid should be focused on debt relief, health and education.

The workshop agreed that unless the context of the international economy is put right, no amount of good aid can help. Therefore: debts should be cancelled, commodity prices improved, northern dumping of produce and of food aid on southern economies should be stopped, tariffs against southern manufacturers should be cut, and there should be more South-South aid such as the Tanzania/Uganda contracts, banks such as the Bank of Bangladesh, Arab aid, and the use of southern experts.

Finally corruption should be strongly controlled, and work should be undertaken to get the capital that has flown out of Africa returned.

The workshop leader was Paul Harrison, author of *The Greening of Africa* (Paladin, 1987). He has written much about countries throughout Africa, including *The Greening of Lesotho* written in 1990 in response to a request from the King of Lesotho to take a hard look at the effects of aid on that country.

The conference workshops created a forum for lively and informed debate amongst a spectrum of voices ranging from academics to the grassroots

Photo courtesy: Ken Mears

Photo courtesy: Pete Brabban/Oxfam

AFRICAN WOMENS' MOVEMENTS

As a result of historical forces, African women created their own organised movement in an environment of slavery and colonialism and all the subsequent forms these took.

They developed specific tools of analysis stemming from this reality, and in the process of struggling to change their situation they have prioritised their agenda in the best ways that they could to address the issues facing them.

The development of African womens' movements in Africa points to differences with the feminist ideology in Western countries, relating to, for example, the role of the predominantly white personnel of aid agencies and their inexperience, the general phenomenon of domination and its evolution, and the discussion about the formation of the Pan-African Women's Movement and global movement.

Many African women's groups already address key African and global issues. Some represented at the Conference included:

(a)   African Women's Welfare Group: assists women from Somalia, Eritrea, Angola, Zaire, Mozambique, and women arriving from Muslim countries with no family networks to adapt to their new environment, including housing, social security and schooling needs.

(b)   Zimbabwe Women's Action Group: assists women in Zimbabwe through the formation of a pressure group to

"'Culture' is often used as a patriarchal weapon, hampering women's struggle for their rights"

change legislation to favour equal opportunities and contribution to the publication "The Zimbabwe Woman in Law and Development".

(c)   Womankind Worldwide: assists programmes worldwide such as a revolving loan fund of £1,000 for women farmers in Ghana.

(d)   The Tigray Women's Association: aims to improve communication between women in Tigray and to build a support network with those in the UK. Its role in rural areas particularly is to strive for land and political and economic rights for women without childcare or education facilities.

(e)   Zimbabwe Welfare Society: works to create awareness of issues in Zimbabwe, providing assistance to women who remain disillusioned with the lack of progress since independence.

(f)   Women's International League: aims to establish contact with existing women's groups in Africa.

Women do not always join womens' groups, sometimes preferring others which are seen to have "more influence". The conclusion, however, was that policies formulated by outsiders, such as men from patriarchal backgrounds who do not, or do not want to understand their oppression of women, are ineffective.

Women have always met each other and been aware of issues concerning their lives and choices. However, "culture" is often used as a patriarchal weapon, hampering womens' struggle for their rights, for example in the case of certain Islamic leaders denying women their rights. Class as a means of economic empowerment for middle class women helps them escape from their dependency on their husbands or male relatives. However, in Africa women are still largely dependent on men for financial survival and social acceptability. Empowerment can, and has, been gained by group formation and support for other women. A global movement would speed up this process.

By not being allowed to talk about many subjects women lose power over what happens to their children and their own bodies. The breakdown of extended family systems in Africa has eroded a system of family welfare. Men have encouraged an image of the "super woman" which now means that women work as well as look after their husbands and families. If they fail to cope with this huge workload they are made to feel they are failures.

Solutions must be founded on sustainable models in the long term, but in the short term every effort must be made to avoid past "solutions". Confidence for women to build alternatives for themselves, be they refuges to flee to or economic support, will come from campaigns for democracy and the creation of welfare states throughout Africa.

It was agreed to form a Womens' Group to continue this discussion and act upon the above issues, and that Oxfam should be asked to help with arranging the first meeting.

The workshop leader was Fatima Babiker Mahamoud, who through her teaching and writing is an advocate of Womens' liberation globally, and in Africa in particular. Involved for the last 27 years in the Womens' Trade Union and political movement for womens' rights in Sudan, she is presently President of the Association of Sudanese Academics and Researchers (UK), advisor to Africa World Review, and Associate Professor of Political Economy and Development at South Bank University, London.

Reading a copy of *Workers' Challenge* in the Resources Centre at the Oxfam office in Lusaka. *Workers' Challenge* is a bi-monthly tabloid with a print-run of 16,000 per issue

Photo courtesy: Robert M Davies

WORLD PRESS CENTRE - EQUAL NEWS ACCESS FOR AFRICA

The World Press Centre is a global computer clearing house on the internet enabling journalists, policy-makers, and grassroots organisations to communicate and receive the latest African news source material relevant to specific matters. The aim is to use this technology to ensure that fundamental policy questions for Africa are fully aired.

The Africa News consists of three types of new and current material:

Agenda: including forthcoming press conferences, events, visitors, publications and speeches

News: including releases of the day

Background: including information on each source, and background profiles and information on regions and policies.

The Africa Service will focus material on African policy matters by a news calendar in the following areas:

☐ Economic policy: structural adjustment, poverty, trade, exchange rates, taxation, etc

☐ Finance: development funding, multilateral debt, foreign investment

☐ Business: industry, manufacturing, mining, tourism, transport, informal sector

☐ Human settlement: refugees, urbanisation, housing, land rights

☐ Development: donors, aid policy, rural, institutions, infrastructure

☐ Regional Cooperation: OAU, ECOWAS, PTA, SADC, African Economic Community

☐ International Relations: UN & Africa, South-South cooperation

☐ Science and Technology: research, appropriate technology, telecommunications, information technology

☐ Water and Sanitation: resources, quality, droughts/floods, fishing

☐ Oceans: ports/trade, coastal zone management, conservation

☐ Environment: energy, forests, wildlife, climate change, pollution, desertification

☐ Women, Children, Family: labour, rights, population, religion, culture

☐ Health: care, mortality, resources, preventative, treatment, training, AIDS

☐ Education: literacy, informal, women, training, empowerment

☐ Agriculture & Food: research, security, imports/aid, exports, prices, pests

☐ Governance, Democracy, Conflict: military, elections, media freedom, human rights, participation, priorities, ethnicity.

Material from official, voluntary, business and research sources is accessible by policy subject area, region, country or city. Steering Groups advise the World Press Centre on Africa coverage, drawing on members from non-governmental, media, business, research and campaigns sectors.

WPC is available by subscription, with special rates applying to African users, from 3 Parolles Rd, London N19 3RE, phone 071 263 6331, fax 071 281 2866, internet address wpc @ wpc.co.uk

The workshop was run by Peter Thompson and Bernard Woods. Peter Thompson is an economist and journalist, presently Director of the World Press Centre. His work to investigate how to make the development community's public information more accessible to journalists started in 1985, backed by Oxfam, Christian Aid and Band Aid. Bernard Woods is Director of CTD Ltd UK, author of *Communication, Technology and the Development of People*, and formerly Senior Communications Specialist at the World Bank.

Talent and hopes of the future imperiled by Zambia's massive debt

Photo courtesy: Ken Mears

AFRICAN DEBT

Discussion began with questions such as: should the International Monetary Fund provide finance to compensate for the adverse terms of trade facing African countries?; should surplus countries, such as Japan, contribute at concessional rates? There was also recognition that the African debt crisis is compounded by problems of environmental degradation and hence sustainable development now assumes critical importance.

There is a need for a strongly African development agency rather than for a super-national agency. There is a need to create mass markets, but how are African incomes to be raised as well? African governments should focus efforts on creating employment opportunities. The roles of the IMF and World Bank have become too intrusive, involving rolling back the sovereign state and ignoring internal social factors. The net transfer of resources from Africa to northern governments and banks, with the accompanying extraction of resources, is unsustainable. Do we expect too much interest from our high street banks who have to squeeze Africa for the extra 1/2% on our deposit accounts?

Achieving macro-economic stability conflicts with micro-economic poverty alleviation. Development itself requires people's participation which means reforming, not abolishing the state and corrupt governments. People's access to power, and state accountability need to be linked, enabling social justice and growth to be achieved through social economics which do not see the state/market split as a polarised "either/or" problem.

Research into the creation of viable infrastructures in newly independent countries will help to draw conclusions about where aid should be given on the basis of identified needs, not on the "political correctness" of countries. The World Bank's role might become one of guarantor rather than funder.

"The IMF and World Bank have become too intrusive, involving rolling back the sovereign state and ignoring internal social factors"

Even if debt were to be written off, the challenges of development would remain, requiring self-help and self-management strategies in each country. Encouragement of regional cooperation within Africa would reduce the dependency on the North. Economies would need transforming from their agriculturally orientated base, while recognising constraints such as the role of the state in infrastructure - creating conditions for change, access to decision making, etc - as well as global and national conditions.

Radical changes within states would need to empower the poor and bring about genuine democratic governance in countries. The Organisation of African Unity could be the basis for harnessing appropriate cooperation.

The key prospects for achieving change remain campaigning within Europe and Africa to change the direction of current thinking, and creation of pressure groups around issues such as GATT, EU relations, the Common Agricultural Policy, and making the World Bank accountable to people. The transfer of information technology and diversification of the African economy will be the means by which macro development objectives will be met in the longer term.

The workshop leader was Dr Sumit Roy, Senior Visiting Fellow at the Department of Economics, City University, London. He has worked on debt and adjustment as Senior Economist at the International Labour Organisation. He is co-author of *Development Experience since 1945* **(Edward Elgar, 1993) and author of** *Agriculture and Technology in Developing Countries: India and Nigeria* **(Sage, 1990). His paper** *Aspects of Structural Adjustment in West Africa and South East Asia* **appeared in the Economic and Political Weekly, September 1993.**

REFUGEES AND DISPLACED PEOPLE

Conflict and refugee issues rely on three key debates. First, the "dialectic of control" which involves how the mobilisation of resources of the so-called "powerless" or "victims" can bring about change: it is important to note refugees are not just victims. Secondly, the "play of probability and chance" remains a dynamic process where outcomes often differ from initial goals. Thirdly, the "problem of reintegration" posing the question "do we really want the status quo?"

The development of "myths" around war often means changing relationships between individuals and the state fail to be addressed. The impact of war on the state often arises from the collapse of dominant society structures, which are replaced by innovative, new social arrangements created in response. Such forces can be utilised in the rebuilding of the state where the "dispossessed" realise their potential in difficult circumstances. However, there are also subsequent struggles between the "haves" and the "have-nots" when the dispossessed do not wish to give up their new-found powers and the ruling class do not wish to give up control.

Rebuilding from the resources of the dispossessed will mean rethinking the concepts of state and society.

Other challenges are associated with the realities of internally displaced people who do not have the same recognised "rights" as refugees. Displacement occurs for political, economic or developmental reasons, linked to the related concepts of democracy, human rights, and trade. How can we interfere, and should we

"Refugees are not just victims. Rebuilding from the resources of the dispossessed will mean rethinking the concepts of state and society"

"Racism in the UK media is fuelled by the fact that 80% of refugees come from 'poorer' countries, worsened by refugee laws copied from Europe with their implicit xenophobia"

interfere, with internal issues facing countries? To whom are we accountable? Where are our priority criteria?

Women suffer particularly within patriarchal structures by being pushed further and further away from the land, leading to loss of state protection and to a loss of personal protection. The solutions are not simple. People are individuals with different needs. Refugees and displaced people display tremendous courage. For some - women, for example - becoming a refugee may be liberating.

In the UK the role of the media is critical, particularly in the debate around immediate relief versus long term effect. Racism in the UK media is fuelled by the fact that 80% of refugees come from "poorer" countries. Difficulties of labelling are worsened by refugee laws copied from Europe with their implicit xenophobia. The issue must be challenged nationally. However, when we speak up the system knows it is being watched and becomes more cautious politically.

The need for internationalism requires host countries, with a changed role for the United Nations High Commission for Refugees, creating and sustaining capacity. The challenge to the global community is based on the role of education - giving people the tools to argue with. The premise must be the freedom for all people to move. We need to define the long-term view which might then drive the short-term. Finally, who are "we"?

The workshop leaders were Monica Kathina and Mark Chingono. Monica Kathina at the time of this workshop was Visiting Research Fellow at the Refugee Studies Programme, University of Oxford, UK. She is presently teaching at the Centre for Refugee Studies, Moi University, Eldoret, Kenya. Mark Chingono, at the time of this workshop was a researcher on War and Development in Mozambique at Cambridge University. He is now Research Officer at the Refugee Studies Programme, University of Oxford.

DEMOCRATISATION IN AFRICA - SERVING WHOSE INTERESTS?

Western democracies have evolved democratic systems based on individual rights, whereas African countries tend to rely on community rights as the roots of democratic society. In France, the French Revolution was effected by a middle class. The history of colonialism, however, in for example, Nigeria, Zimbabwe, Kenya and South Africa, imposed external democratic structures based less on class and more on "settlers" and administrative rights.

Until living standards reach a certain level there will be an inevitable emphasis on development over democracy. The interests of international companies and institutions will prevail over peoples' search for authentic rights.

"Multi-party" systems are only a small component of democracy. The right to organise is an essential prerequisite, but within it also lies the differentiation between personalism (i.e. individual) rights versus the collective. Collectivism should be recognised as an essential right, making the community supreme, creating a structure within which democratic groups can operate.

"Democracy is not new to Africa!"

The distinction between community and "the majority" is important as the majority can form a tyranny. Indigenous pre-colonial democratic management practices worked, but on smaller scales. Democracy is not new to Africa! What is new is the conditionality related to democracy in tying, for example, aid and debt concessions

"There are double standards at play in defining democracy. Is the UK itself democratic?"

to the imposition of recognised "western" models of democracy on African countries. The UK Government has lead the move to make aid conditional on democracy, but should the UK then sell arms to Indonesia? Is the UK itself democratic?

There are double standards at play in defining "democracy". The UK's erosion of labour rights and collective bargaining is being taken up by the International Confederation of Free Trade Unions. General Aideed is hunted on one hand, while Savimbi is treated with felt gloves on the other. While some countries agree to conditionality but fail to enforce agreements, others have clearly reached democratic status by the application of international pressure.

At a financial level the role of undemocratic corruption should be exposed honestly. Structural adjustment is undertaken without consulting of the people. Western motives are not democratic: people are kept in poverty and are set against their own governments as a result. In some countries, however, corruption is largely reduced by high standards of education.

"Western democracies have evolved democractic systems based on individual rights, whereas African countries tend to rely on community rights as the roots of democratic society"

Democracy is itself a middle class Christian construct. Religious movements, such as Islamic fundamentalism, sometimes become the only alternative to dictatorial governments. The body politic within some Islamic states is also corrupt.

Democracy relies on a balance of power and rights, such as are being debated in Uganda at present. Bills of Rights must be balanced against executive and judicial powers. Across Africa, the Declaration of Human Rights is often a closely guarded secret (as it is across the world!).

What form should political rights take? Multi-party systems in Nigeria, Uganda, Kenya, Latin America and elsewhere have not been particularly successful. One prerequisite might be a strong middle class, with independent means of support. When people have no alternative they use weapons for generating income. Democracy is a process which takes various forms to which we are all committed, but democratic culture is the essential common element that must be propagated globally.

The workshop leader was Abdul Rahman Babu. In the 1950s he was part of the liberation struggle in East Africa, specifically Zanzibar. After independence in Zanzibar he was Minister for Foreign Affairs and Trade. Following union with Tanganyika to form Tanzania, he was the Minister for Economic and Social Planning for eight years. Following political changes he became a political detainee for six years. After release he went to the US to teach at Berkley and San Francisco State University and then in Amhurst College, Massachusetts. He is now living in the UK, working as the correspondent for Pacific News Service of San Francisco. He also lectures at Birkbeck College.

Voting Power: the first votes on Eritrea's secession from Ethiopia were cast by disabled former Eritrean soldiers.

Sarah Errington/Panos Pictures

DISABILITY

It is estimated that 10% of people in Africa are disabled. Disability is a vital liberation struggle. Having been defined historically by able bodied people and now redefined by disabled people it must be seen in a social context, not as impairment. Society, not the individual, has to change for equality to be achieved. For example, the solution to inaccessible housing is not to house people in institutions but to improve accessibility.

Disabled people have been ignored as part of development and social policy. Change is being brought about by disabled Africans themselves, acting through their own organisations as a force for social change and empowerment of disabled people.

There are many grassroots organisations of disabled people across Africa. Joseph Malinga, banished and institutionalised as a child, managed to establish a very strong southern African movement for disabled people. In Zimbabwe disabled women have set up their own mill, selling products on the open market. In Kampala the Disabled Business People's Association were so successful on a plot of land leased by the city council that they leased their own land, creating a rotating loan scheme, and gaining places on the local authority.

The Self Help Association of Paraplegics in Soweto formed a factory and challenged local prejudices by starting mobility projects. The South African Federation of Disabled People have two lawyers and three workers giving travelling seminars for disabled people and government officials. They seek to influence legislation, and in 1992 Zimbabwe and Zambia started Equal Opportunities Programmes. A fund administered by disabled people has been set up by the Tanzanian government. Methods of fundraising, as well as lists of suitable funders, are held by ORAP (Organisation of Rural Associations for Progress) in Zimbabwe. Empowerment and development need to come from disabled people themselves, with allies.

These democratic and cost-effective innovative solutions initiated by disabled people also have a relevance for other groups seeking to be active and integrated members of their societies and are an important contribution for all countries to the ways forward on social policy. There are undoubted lessons to be learnt in the North from solutions found by disabled people in the South.

African disabled people face discrimination from oppressors, medical and rehabilitation experts, and charities. They are the poorest of the poor everywhere. This situation cannot be left - the numbers of disabled people are growing - because of war, disease, increased ageing and industrialisation. There is a need for an increased growth in disabled peoples' organisations and for them to be part of the global network of disabled peoples' organisations.

Restrictions on lobbying and direct action, lack of clear social policy packages that address self-determination and self-help, lack of information that allows people to make informed choices, and the erosion of state provision of services due to debt servicing make campaigning on disability difficult in many African countries. There are also barriers between those who experience sensory as opposed to physical disability. The needs of the mentally ill, particularly in refugee camps and those caught up in conflict, are rarely addressed, although some work has begun to treat trauma victims in war zones.

Disabled people's priorities are:
- [ ] identifying forms of oppression;
- [ ] equalisation of opportunities;
- [ ] liberation of the individual through income generation;
- [ ] the need for rehabilitation in the community, not in institutions.

"Disability is a vital liberation struggle"

In addition, information should be made accessible and far-reaching across Africa.

The workshop leaders were Rachel Hurst and Agnes Fletcher. Rachel Hurst is Project Director of Disability Awareness in Action. Through membership of Disabled Peoples' International and as a Trustee of Action on Disability and Development she has been involved with disabled people in Africa for many years, with a special interest in disabled womens' issues. Agnes Fletcher is information officer of Disability Awareness in Action, and a writer and activist in the disability movement.

"Disability was defined historically by able bodied people and now is redefined by disabled people. Society, not the individual, has to change for equality to be achieved"

Workshop leader Rachel Hurst, Project Director of Disability Awareness in Action (right), listens to a point from a workshop participant

Photo courtesy: Ken Mears

ARMED CONFLICT IN AFRICA

Conflict in African states can be caused by a number of factors in varying combinations - religious, cultural, ethnic, tribal, uneven development, liberation by proxy, artificial political boundaries, and internal power relations. However, the root causes lie in fragile ecological, social and economic structures.

The armed conflicts which have afflicted Africa over the last three decades have usually been interpreted as typical ethnic-tribal and/or religious-cultural conflicts. While these categorisations may have served as plausible descriptions of earlier conflicts, and may still have some bearing on how current conflicts are being conducted and perceived, the reality is that conflicts are historical processes, not static events, and so their causes tend to change and diversify over time.

During the last three decades serious ecological transformations have taken place all over Africa. Prolonged and severe climatic desiccation, coupled with intensive exploitation of soil, forest and other natural resources, as well as huge increases in the human and livestock populations, have so degraded the inherently fragile environment of the continent that conflicts caused or catalysed by these compounding ecological factors were bound to take place.

In fact, ecological degradation has been so severe that the traditional means for the prevention and management of inter-ethnic disputes, for example the Tuareg and Fur conflicts in Mali and Sudan respectively, have been rendered virtually unworkable. Indeed it is remarkable that many of the current disputes are not being fought

FARMING IN RWANDA BEFORE THE WAR: Since the spring of 1994, in Oxfam's largest ever emergency relief programme, over £10 million has been spent to support Rwandan refugees in the neighbouring countries of Burundi, Uganda, Tanzania, Zaire as well as in Rwanda itself.

Vincent Barabakintu/Oxfam

along traditional political borders, but along ecological borders that divide richer and poorer ecozones, for example in the civil wars of Chad and Sudan. This has highlighted the need for qualitative development of the traditional methods of conflict management and resolution to enable the parties to deal effectively with this new and unprecedented predicament.

To continue to treat all conflicts in Africa as purely ethnic, tribal, political or religious, and to ignore the growing impact of ecological degradation and depletion of the resource base, could ultimately lead to a distorted understanding of the real situation, and consequently limit the possibility of genuine conflict resolution.

"The armed conflicts which have afflicted Africa over the last three decades have usually been interpreted as typical ethnic-tribal and/or religious-cultural conflicts. However, the root causes lie in fragile ecological, social and economic structures"

Africa's environment is the most fragile of all the continents. The past three decades has seen the delicate equilibrium upset, particularly in the vast arid and semi-arid areas of the Sahel and the Horn of Africa. Persistent drought and unsustainable methods of land use, such as large-scale mechanised rain-fed farming and overgrazing in marginal lands, are destroying the life support ecosystems of these vulnerable regions. Millions of people have been forced to abandon their homelands and become refugees or internally displaced. The result of the competition for dwindling resources is social turbulence and armed conflict.

In addition, members of the African elite, prompted by their assimilation into the world market in the restricted role of extractors of primary resources, are accelerating the unprecedented industrial extraction of resources. Loan conditionalities imposed by the World Bank and the IMF have considerably pushed the restructuring of Africa's resource utilisation away from local needs and moved the local market towards the demands of the international market.

In the past, people in distress simply moved to a nearby richer ecozone. However, this option is increasingly being hampered by population density, large-scale mechanised farming, and political and ethnic tensions. The movement of people and herds from one affected ecozone to another area already occupied by a different ethnic group is a recipe for tension and hostility. Conditional agreements used to be reached when the need for sharing the land was occasional, but now that the need is for prolonged periods or even permanent sharing, the strains are much greater.

Over-exploitation of countries by elites has lead to 80% of land in some countries being owned by absentee landlords. Equal economic sharing is important, both by forms of African socialism, and by traditional African sharing.

The workshop was lead by Dr Mohamed Suliman, Coordinator of the Institute of African Alternatives, where he has established an Environment Unit. He previously lectured at the University of Khartoum.

Dr Mohamed Suliman, Coordinator of the Institute for African Alternatives, in lively debate with workshop participants

Photo courtesy: Ken Mears

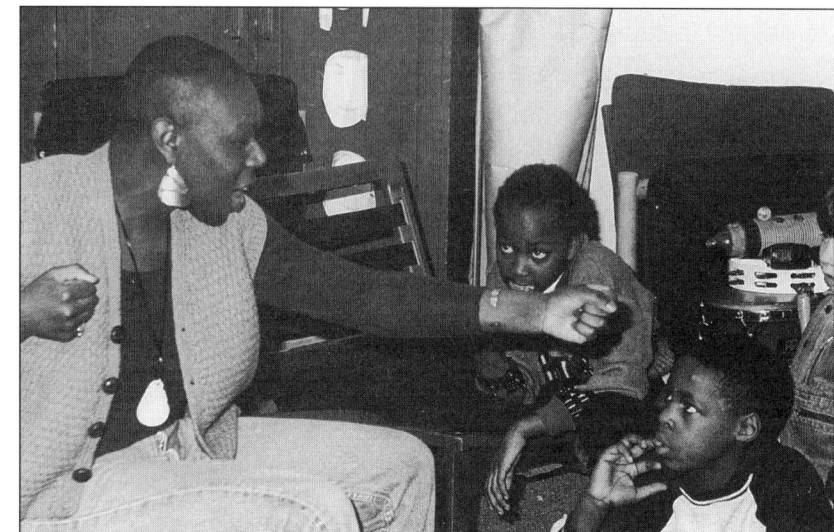

The conference creche was an opportunity to experience African traditions of storytelling and music-making

Photo courtesy: Ken Mears

AFRICAN LITERATURE AND DEVELOPMENT

The lack of publishing companies which can provide a fair quality product in most regions in Africa means that many authors have to go outside the continent to have their work published. Books stocked by schools and libraries are of very poor quality, with a reliance on books sent from western countries containing out of date information, and based on racial images and racist language.

The political climate in many African nations forces writers into exile or prison resulting in an internal ideological vacuum. The cultures of many nations are the poorer for the loss of such voices, as are the pro-democracy struggles. The rise of both Christian and Islamic fundamentalism has also had an oppressive, constricting effect on what can be written or published, in particular on the gender dimension, resulting in women writers suffering more than their male counterparts.

There is a need for establishing more writers' cooperatives to enable writers to publish their own work, something that in reality is difficult in many areas where adverse political conditions exist. Funding and support from international groups is required.

All cultural forms - literature, drama, music and dance - are in danger of becoming more orientated to the expectations of western tourists. There has always been a connection between literature and development, with a particularly strong connection between African writers and the anti-slavery struggles. The role of literature in

"Culture reflects experience. Governments will not empower writers as they are dangerous, reflecting traditions which may not be welcome"

"There has always been a connection between literature and development"

reflecting the new-found African confidence, and in influencing anti-colonial struggles, remains important.

African literature has not arisen in the form of "literature for literature's sake", but more often in the context of critical commentary on governmental and social issues. Nevertheless, there are also "leisurely" and popular forms of literature.

Writers need to address a number of questions:
- [ ] who are they writing for? - western markets, with the attendant cultural distortions that this brings?
- [ ] do they reflect the "real life" of the country?
- [ ] does writing in exile mean that you have to love your cultural identity? - it can be useful to write about culture from different perspectives, from outside your homeland.

Although writing is inevitably personal some writers become symbols of a struggle, liberation or in other political contexts.

Publishing, though apparently collapsing in some areas, is nevertheless strong in, for example, Zimbabwe or South Africa. In other countries too great a value is put on publishing reviews, secondary school level materials, etc, whilst non-school book texts are decreasing.

"The role of literature in reflecting the new-found African confidence and in influencing anti-colonial struggles remains important"

Culture reflects real experience. Governments will not empower writers as they are dangerous, reflecting traditions which may not be welcome. Children's education must be culturally relevant, especially if it is in a foreign language such as English. Women's writing is also critical in challenging their romanticised status in history and literature.

The workshop was lead by Dr Olu Oguibe, winner of the 1992 Christopher Okigbo All-Africa Prize for Literature, recipient of the jury's honourable mention for the 1993 Noma Award for Publishing in Africa. He teaches critical theory at Goldsmith's College, London, and works as Europe Bureaux Chief of the American World. He is also on the management committee of the Africa Research and Information Bureau (ARIB) London, an umbrella organisation of African refugees and immigrants in the UK.

MOZAMBIQUE AND ANGOLA

There are very few instances of in-depth coverage of these countries in the UK press, with the exception of Victoria Britain in *The Guardian*, and papers such as *Caribbean Times (incorporating African Times)* and other black press.

In Angola, after the liberation struggle and independence in 1975, major advances had been made in health care, literacy and education. However, the destabilisation carried out by UNITA (backed by South Africa and the USA), and South African direct military incursions and supply provision to UNITA eroded the effects of such progress.

Following the MPLA's election to power under internationally-observed elections in September 1992, UNITA refused to accept the result despite a massive turn-out and a clear majority for the MPLA. They went on a military rampage, extending the territory they controlled from 20% to 60-70%. The UN has described it as "the worst war in the world," with a death toll estimated at a thousand per day, many of them children dying for want of medicines, water and food in towns beseiged for months by UNITA's armies. Three million refugees have fled UNITA areas, whilst UNITA have defied an increasingly forceful series of UN resolutions condemning their aggression, and are even evading formal sanctions on arms, ammunition and fuel.

"In Angola, after the liberation struggle and independence in 1975, major advances had been made in health care, literacy and education"

In light of the UN's slow response, campaigning action has aimed to achieve the total isolation of UNITA, research the roles of South Africa and Zaire, track down funds from the illicit sale of diamonds, and improve coordination, networking and NGO consortiums working on regenerating community-based development.

In Mozambique the Renamo forces, created by the Rhodesian Intelligence Services, taken over and "upgraded" by the South Africans in 1980, have similarly worked to erode the progress made by the Mozambican government after independence. The prime aim of this destabilisation process has been to destroy the national aim of conquering underdevelopment in the fields of literacy, primary health care and other sectors.

Multi-party elections originally timetabled by the UN for October 1993 have twice been delayed. Delaying tactics have largely characterised the style of the Renamo negotiating team. After two years of responsibility for the effective implementation of the 1992 agreement, Onumoz (the UN operation in Mozambique) have been accused by various observers of being biased towards Renamo and insensitive to the judicial and administrative institutions of President Chissano's government.

For many, the peace process has come to symbolise more than just a transition to western-style democracy. Mozambique's colonial legacy and its long-standing relationship of dependency on South Africa continue to condemn it to the sufferings and indignities of international interference in the affairs of a nation state. The current struggle between the state and Renamo is proving to be an isolating experience for the government. To some observers, the elections are merely a victory for South Africa's strategy of destabilisation in the region. Alternatively, the breaking down of the old order in South Africa under an ANC government could be the pivotal shift for politics in the region: a shift which may enable Mozambique to flourish economically whilst also respecting the sovereignty of a democratically-elected government.

The presence of foreign NGOs in the desperate situations which have prevailed in Mozambique has not always had a positive impact. Money sometimes changed hands illegally and affluent lifestyles have contradicted the poverty they sought to address.

Current priorities in the country's programmes for reconstruction and development include the rehabilitation of orphans and other war-affected children, many of whom remain traumatised by their experiences, preferably through gradual reintegration into the community.

The workshop called for support for the Mozambique Angola Committee, as they continue to carry out a range of work, from lobbying internationally to ensuring public education and awareness on the issues involved.

The workshop was lead by Councillor Peter Brayshaw, Co-Chair of the Mozambique Angola Committee since 1990. With Bob Hughes MP, he has jointly chaired the Angola Emergency Campaign since its inception, and has taken part in two delegations to Baroness Chalker, Minister for Overseas Development

Lichinga children's playgroup, including children orphaned by Renamo.
Photo: Keith Bernstein/Oxfam

**Underground
mechanical loader with
apprentice operator
and trainer**

Photo courtesy: Ken Mears

MINING IN AFRICA

Minewatch is a global network of over 100 groups, mostly community-based groups in the South, concerned about the impact of mining, primarily on the environment and indigenous people. It aims to empower local people with information on companies that are encroaching on their land, on polluting mining processes, and by connecting them with other people fighting similar battles. It hopes to co-sponsor a conference in Africa in 1995 involving community organisations, unions, NGOs, environmentalists, experts and small-scale miners.

Mining is not the financial saviour of many African economies. Historically the colonial expropriation of mineral resources has given way to companies and post-independence economic ties. So what are the benefits and who gets them? There are two major trends: first, the large-scale privatisations sweeping across Africa sponsored by the World Bank and others, which follow a political as well as an economic agenda, where "better management" results in cost-cutting often at the expense of African workers. Secondly, there is the increasing interest foreign mining multinationals are again showing in Africa.

"The end of apartheid has allowed the South African mining houses to invest their wealth and technological experience in other countries. This may perpetuate their racist practices and poor union relations"

The end of apartheid has allowed the South African mining houses to invest their wealth and technological experience in other countries. This may perpetuate their racist practices and poor union relations. Other important issues include the need to analyse the relative benefits and problems associated with exploration, mining and rehabilitation of mine sites among the three types of mining - namely large scale (highly capitalised multinational high-tech projects), medium scale (mid-tech, often government sponsored), and small scale (often low-tech involving local people).

"Mining is not the financial saviour of African economies"

Export earnings are seen as a crucial incentive, but reliance on minerals can leave a country a victim of commodity prices, especially if it has to import expensive equipment and fuel for high-tech mines. Sometimes small-scale or informal sector mining is made illegal in order that mine employment is increased in the formal sector. Yet the high-tech mine jobs will often not go to local people, who are displaced by migratory workforces from outside the region or country who may have some previous experience. As noted in Zimbabwe, women are often involved as a way of increasing their income from agriculture. Infrastructural demands of mining can often create lop-sided economies, such as the Zambian copper-belt where power-grids and transport systems converge on mining regions leaving rural areas with no services.

Added environmental factors and the "polluter pays" principle are no guarantee against pollution: corporate mining companies may still find it cost-effective to pollute, using the demand for clean up only to guarantee that rehabilitating large sites, which only they can do, is a chance to make profit out of sanitising their own mess.

Land rights, vital to local people living on the land, are often ignored. There is little or no compensation, and the resulting social and health problems can also be great both for the workforce and local people. In addition, economically, the life-span of mining is very short, with the average mine not lasting more than 20-30 years before becoming exhausted. The problems of decommissioning and rehabilitation, as well as retrenchment of the workforce, are often not addressed.

"Land rights, vital to local people living on the land, are often ignored"

In conclusion, it was agreed by the workshop that small-scale mining could generally be seen as empowering, while large-scale brought disempowerment. If there are benefits in large-scale mining they go to people outside of the area or country mined, and the losses are suffered primarily by those nearest the mine site.

The workshop was lead by Andrew Whitmore, a founding member of Minewatch, currently chair of its Africa Working Group. He has also worked for Survival International.

DEVELOPMENT AID TO TARGET CONFLICT PREVENTION

To the majority of Africans the environment and economy are closely intertwined. The resources rural Africans use for their everyday livelihood such as soil, water, fuel, labour and livestock are obtained from both the environment and the economy. The matrix of human activity for social production is dependent on the available natural resources.

Many Sub-Saharan countries experiencing macro-economic hardships are recipients of aid from major donor countries, international agencies offer multilateral assistance, and NGOs provide and channel charity donations. The interventions have a bias towards income generation within the cash economy. But the way the economy operates, with planning data dictated by aggregates such as Gross Domestic Product (GDP), Gross National Product (GNP), income per capita, etc, is insensitive to the cultural perceptions of micro-ecological and socio-economic problems experienced particularly by the poor, such as water quantity not quality, pasture availability, vertisols for dry season cultivation, and herb enclaves. Modern economics has not as yet come up with adequate quantification of the value of the environmental resources that are used by local people in Africa.

In addition, the market economy, which the poor have to enter through donor/NGO funded projects, does not give the true economic value of local environmental resources nor the indigenous skills required to sustain livelihoods. The emphasis on the part of intervening

"The market economy does not give the true economic value of local environmental resources nor the indigenous skills required to sustain livelihoods"

organisations is mostly in economic terms, with the hope of social benefit spin-offs.

National and international development and aid programmes are often unwittingly part of the process of resource extraction from the weak by the strong. In doing so the programmes stimulate conditions ripe for conflict, especially where one community may be favoured over another, altering the balance of power between ethnic groups. Instead of intervention through projects, effort should be made towards strengthening social cohesion of the kinship support networks, fora for community discussion on development, tax relief for small producers, inter-community information exchange, and rehabilitation of existing production systems.

"National and international development and aid programmes are often unwittingly part of the process of resource extraction from the weak by the strong. In doing so the programmes stimulate conditions ripe for conflict"

Defining deprivation in strictly economic terms rather than in terms of local resources, and promoting short-term economic gain as the development goal, is incompatible with a long-term holistic approach to community development. The introduction of western-designed development programmes has globalised resources and exposed vulnerable communities to the full competition of the international economy.

Changes in the economic, social and ecological background influence the nature of conflicts in Africa, the boundaries of which are fluid and unpredictable. It is justifiable to assume that far-reaching ecological changes have contributed to the nature and expansion of social turbulence among pastoralists, agropastoralists and cultivators. Yet vulnerable communities have for years relied upon their indigenous coping mechanisms to survive, and self-reliance has proved crucial in times of crisis. Development agencies should opt to strengthen traditional community structures for survival and emphasise the resilience of time-tested survival mechanisms.

The practical concern is how development aid can be used to prevent, manage and ultimately resolve potential and actual conflicts. In January 1994 the IMF/World bank inspired a 50% devaluation of the West African franc in West Africa, halving at a stroke the region's natural resources, commodities, livestock, and indigenous skills and making them easy to purchase by the elite linked to the international monetary systems. The elite and western consumers can now obtain African produce and natural resources at a better quality and cheaper price, all at the expense of a degraded production base. Retrenched workers are left to fend for themselves and may find alternatives such as banditry more viable.

In Africa the starving and refugees are victims of an economic greed that we cannot quench.

The workshop leader was Dr William Lume, Researcher for the Institute for African Alternatives.

Two members of the
Zimbabwe Women's
Cooperative display a
rich variety of wares
proving that despite
unfair world trading
structures it is possible
to trade with true
benefit to the
producers - and come
up smiling!

Photo courtesy: Ken Mears

REGIONAL ECONOMIC COOPERATION

The problems of inter-governmental organisations in West Africa (which was the focus region of the workshop) include the reality that there are too many, resulting in duplication of aims and efforts, arrears on subscriptions, lack of qualified staff to run them, political unrest in the region, poor communications and transport networks, and currency problems.

The workshop recommended that:

- ☐ the scope of the Economic Community of West African States (ECOWAS) should be widened to be the main agency for the promotion of economic cooperation and integration as it is currently under-utilised;
- ☐ there should encouragement of integrated investment in infrastructure, education, communications and transportation networks;
- ☐ campaigning should aim to remove unfair trading restrictions, such as rules of origin, to allow African products to compete fairly on the international markets;
- ☐ aid should cease to African countries because of its negative impact in the past.

Economic cooperation and integration are the vital weapons for fighting poverty and economic dependence on the West. ECOWAS should coordinate and harmonise the use of the human and material resources of the sub-region.

"Economic cooperation and integration are the vital weapons for fighting poverty and economic dependence on the West"

The aims of integration should be:

(a)   creation of a sub-regional economy;

(b)   development of infrastructure;

(c)   development of the productive capacities both for the agricultural and industrial sectors;

(d)   improvement of educational and training facilities;

(e)   development and maintenance of information systems.

The participation of people in the process of integration should be facilitated by setting up fora linked to the decision making organisation of ECOWAS. These fora would promote debates on what the people want, sustaining the theme of unity of purpose.

The workshop recognised that political stability and commitment by governments were prerequisites to effective regional cooperation, and that the roles of individuals and organisations such as NGOs in the process of integration and cooperation would involve the need to apply pressure on Western governments and institutions to refrain from using divisive tactics in West Africa and on the African continent as a whole.

The workshop leader was Dr. Ekei Etim, Director of the Pioneer Agency for Development in Africa. She previously lectured on Economics and International Politics at Edo State University, Ekpoma, Nigeria and was Research Officer for the Women's Programme of the Council for World Mission. Her various reports and articles include *African Debt Crisis: Which Way Africa?* (published by CAMEC, London 1991).

Conference debate extended even to the youngest!

Photo courtesy: Ken Mears

TIGRAY
- A NEW HOPE

Tigray in northern Ethiopia has a population of 5 million. About 46% of the people have access to health services but only 19% access to a safe water supply.

The Relief Society for Tigray (REST) is now moving away from relief to development work, having worked with the Tigray People's Liberation Front (TPLF) since the start of war against the former military government. Their work to establish Tigrayan democratic institutions has resulted in an irreversible sense of self-rule throughout Tigray. It is the people who decide about their own affairs, with decisions based on resources. REST believes people should institute their own development programmes, aid being delivered only to locally assessed needs. REST therefore serves only to supplement local work which in the last few years has concentrated on water and soil conservation. Currently it is setting up a Rural Bank.

Tigray suffers from erratic rainfall which has caused recurrent drought and soil erosion. To tackle this problem 75% of all farm land has been terraced and small dams built, but no matter what is done a problem still exists. The land requires a great deal of maintenance work which has to be done manually and there are many difficulties caused by the war and weather still to address.

Now the war is over, Tigray has to work with the central government and national organisations. The relationship between the national and local government is based on a three-tier system, the villages electing representatives at community, regional and national level. Overall responsibility resides in the Central Authority. There are budgetary problems, and the efficiency and efffectiveness of service

Akezd Tirumesh with her baby, building terraces on farmland.
Photo: Jenny Matthews/Oxfam

"It is the people who decide about their own affairs, with decisions based on resources. REST believes people should institute their own development programmes, aid being delivered only to locally assessed needs"

provision at a broader level within Tigray should be viewed in this regional economic context. The provision of services is controlled both locally and nationally. Whilst people control distribution of food aid locally and can assist in the provision of buildings, they are unable to meet the need to provide skilled teachers as well as medical equipment and drugs for clinics, so these responsibilities remain with the central authority. This creates a tension, which the trend towards weaker central control and devolution of power may ease in the future.

At present REST has become a registered charity organisation working in partnership with others such as the Ethiopian Relief Organisation. There is much trading across the newly opened borders, and agricultural production has increased following the scrapping of the fixed but low prices of the old Ethiopian Agricultural Marketing Corporation which had discouraged farmers from producing as much as they could. There is a trend to produce cash crops such as sesame, although cotton production is not yet developed.

State-owned cooperatives, which were established under the former regime have been privatised, and land distribution is more equitable than ever before. However, no development work is initiated without the involvement and active participation of the people of Tigray. There is a need for NGO participation, but NGOs must concentrate on the enablement of people to achieve their own goals. At present a lack of coordination among NGOs causes a loss of resources.

NGOs' roles should now be analysed in terms of their social aspects and impact, such as on employment, rather than by their immediate economic benefits.

The workshop was lead by Dr. Solomon Inquai, Chairperson of the REST Support Committee in the UK. He works for the International Extension College.

HOW TO TAKE CAMPAIGNING ACTION ON AFRICA

Launch of Oxfam's Africa Make or Break Campaign

Photo courtesy: Ken Mears

With the end of the Cold War came an as yet unrealised hope of peace and a new world order. Africa, confronted with a worsened situation, still faces the possibility that its poor will increase from the current 200 million to 300 million in the next six years.

Despite the diagnosis and prescription of Structural Adjustment Programmes now being vigorously implemented in 16 of the 53 states, debt indicators have worsened and arrears keep growing. Sub-Saharan debt totalled US$183 billion which, according to the World Bank, is equivalent to 90% of the Gross National Product of the countries concerned. In most cases debt servicing bills were as high as four times the total expenditure on health.

Former Tanzanian President Julius Nyerere once asked whether we should "starve our children to pay our debts"? He has been answered several hundred times with a "yes". The crushing debt burden is sapping all the savings that may have been used for recovery. Economic conditionalities have no concern for the long-term, such as the way cuts to education budgets will only create new generations of illiterate people who cannot exercise democracy, nor even be useful producers in the future.

Aid and investment should be based on economies that prioritise food security. Hostile trade regimes with commodity prices falling and prices of manufactured goods rising must be stopped. Recovery

"Aid must focus on the poorest people, which means rural populations in many cases, and it should be managed through local community organisations and NGOs, which are more accountable to local people and have the skills and experience"

"Western governments and banks should cancel all debts now, as debt penalises the poorest people first"

is an internal concept, but must be supported, and therefore Africans must promote integrated development programmes which will ensure food security, cessation of conflict, protection of the environment, and building capacity for production.

People should be empowered to demand their basic human rights and services. Five main factors need to prevail to achieve this goal:
- ☐ women's liberative movements;
- ☐ local control over resources;
- ☐ sustainable use of land;
- ☐ emphasis on rural development;
- ☐ effective institutions to provide local credit through low interest, non-exploitative finance.

Aid must focus on the poorest people, which means rural populations in many cases, and it should be managed through local community organisations and NGOs, which are more accountable to local people and have the skills and experience to carry out development programmes. Western governments and banks should cancel all debts now, as debt penalises the poorest people first. Donors are also culpable in arranging loans which cannot be repaid. Conditions attached to aid should be based on how democratic the state is, and its degree of respect for human rights.

"Nyerere once asked whether we should 'starve our children to pay our debts' He has been answered several hundred times with a 'yes'."

Oxfam's campaigning should aim to influence other donor countries to target aid on the poorest, with conditions based on democracy, justice, and sustainable development.

Africans must join their voices to that of the Zambian who said "I urge you, before my starving family dies, scrap all that our nation owes you". Mark that the word is "urge", not "beg". How does Africa "urge"?

The workshop leader was Odhiambo Anacleti, Oxfam Communications Officer for Africa and former Oxfam Coordinator for Africa South and Oxfam Representative for Tanzania. Before that he was a teacher, civil servant and lecturer.

Oxfam Stands for Change: Make a Stand With Us!

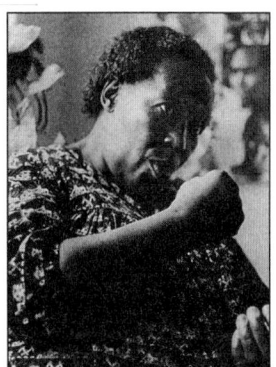

Margaret Nhlapo secretary of the South African Dpmestic Workers Union, who campaigned with Oxfam's support, throughout the apartheid era

Photo courtesy: Oxfam

There is a worldwide network of people linked through Oxfam who are committed to challenging world poverty and its causes. Throughout the apartheid regime Oxfam supported communities campaigning against evictions and organisations like the Domestic Workers' Union who stood up for workers' rights. On the other side of the globe, Saptagram is an organisation of village groups in Bangladesh campaigning for their rights by organising marches and other protests against the increase in violent attacks on women. Amazonian Indian communities are also supported by Oxfam in their campaign for their rights through the Union of Indian Nations, who campaigned at the Brazilian Congress and won the legal rights to their land and prohibition of land exploitation without their consultation.

In the UK, Oxfam campaigners are lobbying their MPs and other decision makers, who right now are setting priorities for the future, to tell them that ending global poverty should be at the top of their list. All over the world ordinary people are fighting poverty, struggling for food, clean water, health care, housing, better working conditions, education, and control over their lives. In 1995 Oxfam launches a major new campaign to assert everyone's entitlement to these and other basic rights and to strike at the international structural causes of injustice and poverty in the world.

If you have been inspired by the insights and determination expressed within this *Tomorrow's Africa* report, please consider how you can help achieve this vision for a fairer world by joining the Oxfam Campaigning Network. You will receive a quarterly newsletter featuring campaign briefings, news and comment, with a section telling you what's going on in your local area. There's an introductory pack with practical campaigning advice and campaigning materials. You can elect to receive urgent action mailings on urgent issues as they arise so you can take campaigning action, and you will get regular updates on campaigns, who's doing what, where, and what we're achieving.

Enoch Samudengo writes to the World Bank. The arrival of his letter and 15,000 others from Zambia rocked the annual meeting of the world bank and IMF

Photo courtesy: Oxfam

Send the form opposite freepost to join the Oxfam Campaigning Network, or to receive information about other ways you can help by ticking the relevant boxes.

I'd like to join the Oxfam Campaigning Network.

Please send my introductory pack.

I enclose my annual subscription fee payable to Oxfam
☐ Waged £8   ☐ Unwaged £5

☐ Please send me information on how to join my local Oxfam Campaign Group

☐ Please send me information on fundraising with Oxfam

☐ Please send me Oxfam's free development education catalogue of materials for teachers

I enclose a donation of £ .... to Oxfam's work

Mr/Mrs/Ms ....

Address ....

....

.... Postcode ....

Telephone ....

Send to:
Oxfam, Freepost, 58 St John's Hill, Clapham Junction, London SW11 1YY

CT/AT/TOMAF   Oxfam is a Registered Charity No. 202918

Other books from Hansib Publishing

Forthcoming titles

PRIDE OF BLACK BRITISH WOMEN
by Deborah King

A book which provides young people, particularly young black people who were born in Britain, with positive images and role models of women who they can relate to, identify with and aspire to emulate.

1 870518 34 9. Pb £5.95

PIONEERS OF PROGRESS
**Legendary figures from Africa, Asia and the Americas
who changed the course of social and political history.
by Christopher Johnson**

This wide-ranging collection of essays introduces the contributions of thirty-eight prominent political thinkers and cultural pioneers from the world's non-European majority.

1 870518 32 2. Pb £7.95

ARISING FROM BONDAGE
A History of East Indians in the Caribbean 1838-1993
by Ron Ramdin
An original work of historical research which not only puts into perspective,
but also evokes, in both scope and depth, the epic story of East Indians in
the Caribbean
1 870518 36 5. Pb £12.95

CORNERED TIGERS
A History of Pakistan's Test Cricket:
From A. H. Kardar to Wasim Akram
by Adam Licudi
The most comprehensive and up-to-date book on Pakistani Test Cricket,
covering the development of the Test team since its inauguration in 1952,
to the present
1 870518 31 4. Pb. £16.95

the modern book of
muslim
NAMES

Zafar Malik

Kashif Ali

HANSIB PUBLISHING

THE MODERN BOOK OF MUSLIM NAMES
by Zafar Malik & Kashif Ali
A reliable and straightforward reference source of over 3000 Muslim
names, with all modern variations and a brief meaning.
1 870518 33 0. Pb £4.95

Recently published

PROSPERO'S RETURN?
Historical Essays on Race, Culture and British Society
by Paul B Rich
A wide-ranging collection of essays exploring the nature and meaning
of race and racism in British society and the nature of British and
English national identity.
1 870518 40 3. Pb. £8.95

ANTIGUA & BARBUDA: A Little Bit of Paradise
(2nd revised edition)
Presenting in a unique style some of the most decisive stages in the
social and economic history of Antigua & Barbuda, giving the reader a
true reflection of the culture and people of this island state.
1 870518 27 6. Hb. £25.00

GRENADA: Spice Island of the Caribbean

This unique country profile presents a complete view of Grenada,
Carriacou and Petit Martinique - combining historical and modern
photographs with authoritative commentary on social and economic
history and the country's abundant natural assets

1 870518 29 2   Hb. £25.00

THE OTHER MIDDLE PASSAGE
Journal of a Voyage from Calcutta to Trinidad, 1858
Introduced by Ron Ramdin
Reproducing, in facsimile, the Journal of the Captain of the 'Salsette',
a ship carrying Indian indentured labourers from India to the West Indies.
1 870518 28 4. Pb. £3.95

A NEW SYSTEM OF SLAVERY
The Export of Indian Labour Overseas 1830-1920
by Hugh Tinker
The first comprehensive historical survey of a hitherto neglected and only
partially known migration- the export of Indians to supply the labour needed
on colonial plantations worldwide, following the legal ending of slavery.
1 870518 18 7. Pb. £11.99

Backlist titles

ETHNIC MINORITIES DIRECTORY

With over 20,000 African, Asian and Caribbean business and social organisation listings, this is the first and only national directory of its kind.
1 870518 90 X. Pb. £40

RASTA AND RESISTANCE
From Marcus Garvey to Walter Rodney
by Dr Horace Campbell

A definitive study of the Rastafarian Movement in all its manifestations.
0 9506664 7 5. Pb. £8.95

SPEECHES BY ERROL BARROW
edited by Yussuff Haniff

A collection of speeches made by the late Barbadian Prime Minister, Errol Barrow, over the past three decades through which we gain an insight into his fight for the regions independent identity and prosperity.
1 870518 70 5. Hb. £10.95

HOGARTH, WALPOLE AND COMMERCIAL BRITAIN
by Dr David Dabydeen

An analysis of Hogarth's radical political critique of corruption.
1 870518 45 4. Hb. £15.95

FORBIDDEN FREEDOM (Third Edition)
The Story of British Guiana
by Dr. Cheddi Jagan

A classic document of anti-colonialist and anti-imperialist struggle from one of the veteran freedom leaders of the Third World.
1 870518 37 3. Pb. £5.95

INDIA IN THE CARIBBEAN
ed. Dr David Dabydeen
and Dr Brinsley Samaroo

A collection of essays, poems and prose by leading Indo-Caribbean scholars and writers, on East Indian history and culture in the Caribbean.
1 870518 00 4. Pb. £8.95/1 870518 05 5. Hb. £11.95

BENEVOLENT NEUTRALITY
Indian Government Policy and Labour Migration to British Guiana 1854-1884
by Dr Basdeo Mangru

A detailed scholarly essay on Indian migration, which, for the first time, studies the Indian background of the indentured labourers.
1 870518 10 1. Hb. £12.95

PASSION AND EXILE
by Frank Birbalsingh

A wide ranging collection of essays that offer an illuminating commentary on the literary and history of the English speaking Caribbean.
1 870518 16 0. Pb. £7.95

INSEPARABLE HUMANITY
by Shridath Ramphal

An anthology of reflections from a champion of Third World issues, and a former Commonwealth Secretary-General.
1 870518 14 4. Hb. £14.95

BARRISTER FOR THE DEFENCE
by Rudy Narayan

A book that seeks to improve the quality of advocacy in the criminal courts.
0 9506664 2 4. Pb. £6.95

FROM WHERE I STAND
by Roy Sawh

A moving autobiography from one of Britain's first black spokesmen.
0 9506664 1 6. Pb. £5.95

KING OF THE CARNIVAL AND OTHER STORIES
by Willi Chen

A collection of short stories from the Caribbean, capturing the pathos and racial comedy of Trinidadian society.
1 870518 12 8. Pb. £5.95

THE OPEN PRISON
A novel by Angus Richmond
The story of a young girl growing up on the estate of her white guardian in British Guiana, who is slowly and painfully awakened to a society in turmoil.
1 870518 25 X. Pb. £4.95

THE WEB OF TRADITION:
USES OF ALLUSION IN V.S. NAIPAUL'S FICTION
by Dr John Thieme
A study of one of the Caribbean's major and most controversial novelists, V.S. Naipaul, who has won several of the world's literary prizes including the Booker Prize.
1 870518 30 6. Pb. £6.95

THIRD WORLD IMPACT (8th Edition)
edited by Arif Ali
The only fully comprehensive work of reference regarding the presence of the visible minorities in all spheres of British life.
1 870518 04 7. Hb. £15.95

THE REGGAE FILES
by Gordon C
A collection of interviews with reggae superstars from Jamaica and Britain who speak about the influence of Jamaican politics.
1 870518 03 9. Pb. £6.95

DOMINICA: Nature Island of the Caribbean
This richly illustrated book captures the little known beauty of this Caribbean country and offers a brief account of its sometimes turbulent history and rich culture.
1 870518 17 9. Hb. £19.95

INDO-WESTINDIAN CRICKET
by Professor Frank Birbalsingh and Clem Shiwcharan
Two illuminating essays about a part of cricketing-tradition that is unique to the Westindies.
1 870518 20 9. Hb. £7.95

100 GREAT WESTINDIAN TEST CRICKETERS
by Bridgette Lawrence with Reg Scarlett

When did Michael Holding publicly condemn the bouncer? Which Westindian batting-star could have played for England? Some of the many less well-known facts to be found in Lawrence's excellent anthology, tracing the rise of Westindian Test cricket from its beginnings at Lord's in 1928, to the "golden era" of the 1980s.

1 870518 65 9. Hb. £14.95

COOLIE ODYSSEY
by David Dabydeen

Dabydeen's second book of poems.

1 870518 01 2. Pb. £3.95

GRASSROOTS IN VERSE

An extensive collection of poetry and verse submitted by the readers of Caribbean Times, Asian Times and African Times newspapers. The selections provided are wholly original and as diverse in tone as in subject matter.

1 870518 13 6. Pb. £6.95

Enquiries

UK: Hansib Publishing Ltd, Tower House, 141-149 Fonthill Road, London N4 3HF. Tel: 0171-281 1191.

UK TRADE: Turnaround Distribution, 27 Horsell Road, London N5 1XL. Tel: 0171-609 7836.

USA: Hansib Publishing (USA), 17498 Tuscan Avenue, Granada Hills, California CA 91344.

CANADA: Hansib Publishing (Canada), 22 Gaslight Crescent, Scarborough, Ontario M1C 3S8.

CARIBBEAN: Hansib Publishing (Caribbean) Ltd, PO Box 2773, St John's, Antigua, Westindies

Book Order Form

Please send me a copy of:

TITLE	PRICE	p&p

UK orders please add £1.50 per book for postage & packing. (Overseas orders add £3.00 per book) Orders over £25 POST FREE

I enclose a cheque/PO/Credit Card details for £ .... (payable to **Hansib Publishing Limited**).

Payment by Credit Card:

☐ **Access**   ☐ **Visa**

Card No. ☐☐☐☐☐☐☐☐☐☐☐☐☐☐☐☐☐☐

Name .... Expiry Date ....

Signature .... Date ....

Cardholders Address ....

....

Delivery Address:

Name (Mr/Mrs/Miss/Ms) ....

Address ....

....

.... Postcode ....

Send to:

Hansib Publishing Limited, Tower House, 141-149 Fonthill Road, London N4 3HF England